Letters to You

Sara Sheehan

Letters to you

This one's for you.

Commencement,

This project I've created is far more intimate than every other. This project comes from the deepest part of my heart and soul. Each piece is exactly how I felt at that moment. This isn't poetry, nor fiction. These are letters to the man I've had a force with since we first spoke. As of right now, it's been four months of knowing each other. It's been four months being friends, best friends. Only did we both decide to make it more, mutually. People will say "that was fast" or quickly say the pace we're moving at is too much. But listen, we're going at the perfect pace we feel is right. And honestly, that's all

4

that matters at this point. Not you, not the

world, not even the people closest to us. I

understand some might be worried, some might

go straight for the "what if this happens" It's

great you care, we wouldn't have it another

other way. But truly, our hearts are where

they're at, and they're not disconnecting

because of the timing and what others believe is

right for us. We've found each other at the

right time. We've grown a beautiful connection,

starting from a pure friendship. Our timing is

right on time, if you'd ask me. God knew what

he was doing when he brought him into my life.

I couldn't have prayed harder for him to listen

to me. God, and the universe, set us on the path

towards each other, and we've just made it real.

Everything feels right, and wholeheartedly,

nothing could feel more right.

Letters to you

May

May 28, 2018 7:00 p.m.

I'm so happy I met you, you've taught me what it's like to be free. What it's like to open your heart and love openly, without caring about anything else. You've inspired me to always love, more. I was always fascinated with mystery's, and you found your way to my life—someone who's soft, but not easily open, that's why I was drawn to you. The way your heart cries to the world, the way you wear your heart on your sleeve and have no clue you're even doing it. Thank you for being such a wonderful friend. I've found comfort in you, I've found parts of me that fit with you. I trust the universe, because it gave me you. I'm not easily open, my shell is where I've always resided—and I believe that can make or break any love or friendship I choose to condition. But you, you showed up, right on time, right when I needed you. I thank you for being you. For being the beautiful soul, you are. I only hope you give the world your heart, no holding back. I see you being someone great one day, someone everyone will love, even if they don't see it at first. I know sometimes you might drown in self-doubt, sometimes you might feel there's more you need to do. But listen, you're doing everything perfectly on time—it's not your fault because not everyone's awake,

it's not your fault people decide to look the

other way. Your love is intense, I've felt a

part of it, but it's intensely beautiful. I

think that's the scariest part. I just want

you to know that nothing you're doing is

wrong, it's not your job to wake up anyone

who's choosing to sleep on you. Those

people will wake up one day and see you,

for who you always were, and that's the key

to it all. You'll always be you. I just want

you to promise me that you'll never change,

never choose to change you because not

everyone is ready to love you. I will always

love you, if that means anything. I will

always celebrate you, I will always show

the world your heart even if it's hard for

you. I'll be your number one fan, because at the end of the day, we all need someone who reassures us on who we are, even if we can't do it ourselves. I just want you to know, that your friendship means the world to me, after losing people in my life who've held my comfort close to them, I get you. Someone who's soft, but not easily open, I'm drawn to you. You'll always be a mystery to me. You'll always be, someone I want more from. But for now, know that, being your friend, has been an honor. I'm so happy to call you my friend.

Knowing you, has been admired,

Thanks for letting me in.

June

June 7, 2018 1:26 a.m.

It's been an hour since I spoke with you, and I'm still over here smiling remembering your face. Your face is my favorite. Your smile makes my heart melt a thousand times over. I could stare at you all day and just fall in love every single time. Something about your face, that's so admirable. And that beautiful smile, is a smile that I will never forget. I find comfort in you, you make me forget about all the pain, all the sadness, you make me feel free. And honestly, that is the scariest thing at the same time. To be in love with a man for almost 4 years, but then I met you. A man, who's strong, who has dreams, who has his life figured out even with self-doubts, you're beautiful. I've been obsessed with saving people my whole life, friends, relationships, I always wanted people to know that my love was real, that my love was strong enough to heal whatever hurt them. I always wanted to be loved in return, the exact way I loved. Sometimes I let my guard down when it came to people loving me back, just a bit of love I ran with and that's where I always went wrong. I've been doing love all wrong for so long, but I've never loved wrong. I always loved the same, unconditionally. That was always the difference. I've had my fair share of disappointments, which ended up my fault in the end, but mistakes are lessons to learn from right? Love is such a big word I've learned, I've learned that love is such a scary place to be, if you're not exactly sure you want to be there. It's crazy, to know how crazy I was to be in love back then, as I look now, and see how love is one of my biggest fears. Because I've given someone all of me, loved them with my whole heart and things still didn't work. I fear real love because I'm terrified to know how it'll feel, I'm terrified to hurt the one I love, and I've already done that once. So, I can't speak on your experiences, but I do feel the reasoning for your decision on not choosing a relationship and finding yourself. I've understood how important it is, to love yourself first and to be happy with your own company. But that was also me for basically my whole life and it doesn't seem to get better. Neither situation checks out for me. I'm at that point in my life where nothing makes sense, and I'm just always confused. I'm not sure what part of life this is, but all I know is I just want to run away and you're the only person who puts ease to the pain. I hate to put the pressure on you, but you are a blessing. You are just, great. You've came into my life and showed me it's possible to be with someone else, you've showed me the parts of me I needed to work on, the parts of my life that needed to be dead and renewed. You've

showed me what it's like to just be free. I
feel that every time we talk, I wish I could
live in that moment forever, then I come
back to reality and realize I'm living a
fantasy, a dream that will never become my
reality. I know I put so much pressure on
you, when it comes to talking and just
everything, but I wish you could meet you, I
wish you could see how amazing you were,
through my eyes. Like every part of you was
made for me. You were made for me. If you
weren't, I don't know why you came into
my life, because honestly that would be the
worst prank of my life. But I know God
sent you my way for reasons. I trust him,
and I trust the universe, they never do
wrong by me. Every time you doubt yourself

I just want to hug you and assure you that you're wonderful and every part of you is someone special, to a lot of people. Your work, your words, are incredible and they're real. You can feel every word, deeply. The ones who can't connect with them, don't let it bother you, you won't be for everyone, and everyone won't be for you. But the ones who are, will always show you the most love and appreciate them. For everyone one who decides to look the other way, another will come your way, it's a process that will forever go on. You can't let the disappointments make you believe you're not good enough. Every time you feel less than you, read your work and I promise you, you'll understand where I'm coming

17

from. I promise you that you'll always be good. I know me reassuring you is probably a joke, considering you've never met me and I'm just utterly obsessed with you, but it's coming from a pure place, my heart. My heart doesn't lie, my heart isn't going to trick you. Whatever hurt I've done, I've accepted and I don't let that burden me for finding love that's meant to fit with me. You are very special to me, very deeply, special. I haven't even met you, we've never been physically connected, but mentally, I've connected to you on a level I couldn't explain. I've found the greatest friend I could've ever asked for, one I've been longing for since I've remembered. I can only hope you're in my life forever, I can only hope you stick around and love me one day. I hope you can handle me for everything I am and still decide to be my friend. I know this is long, and I'm sorry. But I wanted you to know how much you mean to me. I wanted to make you aware of the beautiful soul you are. And yeah, I can be very selfish, and you, are amazing and to be with someone like you would be beyond words. I want you so bad, in every way possible. I know that now. I know that when I meet you. My heart never lies to me, it always shows up when it's needed. I just want you to know, I respect you, and your decision on choosing a different way to find love. I'm a free spirit, I believe everyone should do exactly what they love, *in whatever way they feel makes them happy. I respect you finding who you are and becoming a better everything. I admire you for the motivation you have as a person, the kind of love you not only have for yourself, but for the world. I love your heart, and how you're not afraid to show it. I've never met a soul that was as beautiful as you. It's now 2:02 a.m. And I'm still going, I'm probably rambling at this point, but I've figured I'd go all in or not at all. I believe your soul was meant for me, and I'll wait until the day our souls become one. I believe it's all one sided, and the situation is a complete mess but it's how I feel. The feeling is very powerful and overwhelming at times because I know I'd be sad if it's* never reciprocated, but I'd honestly still be

your friend regardless, and I know that's

enough for me. You've been so great in such

a short period of time. You've taught me so

much, already. I can only imagine going

forward, and learning more about you, it

excites me. Learning the you who made you

into who you are today, learning the you

when you're mad, when you're distant,

when you're the happiest. I want to learn

every part of you and love each part.

Because each part of you made you into the

beautiful person you are today and I'm so

happy I got to witness this person. I'll

always pray for you. I'll always be a friend.

I'll always be here. Don't ever stop smiling.

Don't ever stop showing your heart.

Don't ever stop being you. That's my favorite part. And whenever you're ready, I'll be that 1%. Until then, stay great, stay the way you are, but don't stop growing into someone more beautiful. I love you, very much. I just wrote for over an hour. So now I must sleep, but I just wanted you to know how special you are, to me, even if no one else can see it,

I just hope you can see it.

June 18, 2018 1:26 a.m.

I want to say how creepy it is, that I just started writing at this time, because this is the exact time I wrote your last piece. Except this time, I'm leaving everything on this page. No holding back. However you choose to with take this information will be on you. It could possibly terrify you, completely scare you away, or simply just make you happy. I'm not exactly sure which it will be, but I'm taking a huge chance, and I think maybe it should just be said already. You said it best "I'm only fearless when writing" and that's where I'm going with this. I have no fear putting my heart out on this piece because I know regardless you'll appreciate my words. It's crazy how secure I feel when I write, it's like a huge release right off my shoulders, like everything I let build up inside me come pouring out and everything is very intense when it comes to that. But I'm going to give you all of me right now and I'm not thinking of the outcome, well I am, but honestly, at this point in my life I don't have anything to lose. I met you, I admired you from the moment we spoke, and for some reason I've had this force with you, that kept pulling me in your direction. I would be chilling, minding my own business, yet you'd pop up in my head and

I would just want to have a little convo
with you, regardless of what it was about.
Speaking to you was enjoyable, and it was
amazing how anything we talked about
ever got boring, or annoying. We just
communicated randomly, and then it
became more and more. Half the time, I
made it a thing, I went out of my way to
speak with you. And I'm sorry that I did
that, it was wrong on many levels to want
to talk to you while having a whole
boyfriend, but I found myself hoping you'd
talk to me, hoping to see myself smiling
because of you. I just want you to know
that you were great, it always kept it casual
even when I tried you. When I hinted over
and over but you never gave in. Until I,

like you said gave you no choice and you had to give in. Which again, you didn't. You didn't have to, but for some reason you did. But it's not even that I wanted you on a deeper level, I just really enjoyed our conversations even if they were the dumbest ones, you always made my day, and you still do. I always think to myself, about everything. I don't know how this all happened, I try and try to analyze it and I always come up short. I never seem to truly understand how my life can fall apart but I can't feel a thing. Sometimes I feel terrible, for walking away from someone I loved with everything, who I gave all of me too, until you came into my life and helped me see the parts of my relationship that were

26

not able to be fixed, the parts I never really let bother me, the things I needed to bring light to. I never thought I could see myself with anyone but him, and I guess that's what comfort does to you, and comfort scares me entirely, because everyone always gets comfortable right? But a part of me feels like it's not always possible, I could just be thinking too much. I feel like comfort is good, but limited comfort is good. I haven't had much anxiety since I've been apart from him, I've felt happy. And a part of me feels awful because it's like those 3 years could disappear so fast. Love scares me, and I've never been so terrified of love before, and I know every situation isn't the same, but sometimes it's hard to dig

yourself out the hole you dig yourself in to
believe that in the first place. I'm just
scared to ever love someone again because I
don't ever want to lose that love, that spark
on why the love even came to existence in
the first place. But I've learned that the
way you find the love, and how you created
it plays into it as well. I can't save someone
and expect them to reciprocate the same
love back to me, ever. I can't fix the broken
and hope they can love me with the same
kinds of love because I'm just asking for
disappointment. But honestly, our
relationship wasn't that bad. I don't regret
loving him, I don't regret anything I did.
I'm thankful for being able to be with
someone who did everything he could for

28

me, I just wish he could have loved himself more, wish he could have been in a better place when I met him, maybe things would have worked differently. But I'm a firm believer in everything happens for a reason, and everyone you meet plays a huge part in your life. So, I've accepted our fate and I must move forward. I must make peace with it all, and I'm still trying. Thank you for helping me through it, talking to me even when you didn't have to. Always being an open ear and listening to me ramble on how much of a fool I was. You really are an outstanding friend. (Starting to cry now, starting to get real intense). You've helped me see me for who I lost years ago, you've brought me back to life.

29

And I know to you that might sound extremely crazy, because we've never met, and you'll probably feel as you did nothing, but you did. I'm more in tune with my emotions now after I met you then I've been in the last 4 years. Writing has helped me also, but I feel very close to you, as you said, it's like I've known you for years and that's honestly how it feels. Maybe you're my "past life lover" maybe our souls were connected somehow before, and the universe is bringing us together in this lifetime. Or maybe I'm just crazy and you're just great at being wonderful. You've made me feel beautiful in my own skin, something I've never felt ever, growing up dealing with terrible skin, to having people completely turn me down because my skin "wasn't perfect" really has crushed my securities. I haven't once thought about wearing makeup, I've loved my skin and I feel like it's been so beautiful. Maybe because I'm actually happy, but I thank you for just telling me honestly, knowing you always give an honest opinion really made it easier. You've helped me overcome my biggest insecurity and I don't know how to thank you. I know sometimes you probably think you've done nothing, and what I do for you is so much. But the littlest things mean the most to me, and something so small means so much and goes a long way with me. Your friendship has guided me in the direction I was scared to

take in my life. You've given me the
courage to move forward, to be secure, to be
happy with myself. I must work on it,
everyday but thank you for helping me see
me again. And that's why I wish I could
just give you my heart, but instead I'll show
you my heart over and over, openly, not just
because you've been great to me, but
because you're great and you deserve the
world. You deserve to have everyone love
you. You deserve to have your book sales to
be over 393848293. Because you are
THAT great. I know you drown in self-
doubt a lot, but don't we all? There's going
to be times you wake up and take the day
off on a bad start and wish to restart but
understand that you will overcome that bad

day. You will make it to tomorrow. The
universe throws us challenges and
sometimes it's hard to pass them, but you
will, and once you understand that every
bad thing is only temporary, you'll be able
to fully be happy with everything. I know
you know you're amazing, and you believe
it. Don't beat yourself up because not
everyone sees it, focus on the ones who love
it, the ones who go out their way to show
their love for your work, those are the ones
who matter. I know it's hard to just accept
because they're just words, and when self-
doubt hits, everything is unreachable, but
honestly it's just a thought created by your
own mind, and you can shut it down every
time. You don't have to let it control you.

Just remember, you are amazing, your words are beyond beautiful. Your work is intensely raw because it's a piece of you formed into such beautiful words. Some people might relate, some might just enjoy your work—and some might never read. But not everyone will be someone you want around you, not everyone is good, and be thankful for the universe separating the two. I try not to tell you how much I love your work because I know you think I'm lying half the time, just to make you feel good. But I put it on everyone I love, in my family, that your work is best work I've ever read, and I put that over my work as well.

You speak with soul and you can feel everything even if I can't relate, I can feel you put your heart out on each page and to

me that's exactly what it takes to be

someone beautiful. You're naturally

beautiful. I don't know how God created

someone who was so perfect. I sit back and

just think about you, and how perfect you

are, and I get upset thinking you don't see

it too. I just wish you knew. I hope this

makes you realize. I promise I'm not

bullshitting, I mean every single word I'm

putting on this piece. No takes back. I'm

giving you my whole heart right now. I find

you to be a welcoming soul who wants to

help everyone you can possible, and that's

beautiful. Who you are is just beautiful.

I've never met you in person and I feel like

I've met you a thousand times. I love how

you don't care what anyone thinks, how free you are. And how even though you say you're not ready for love, deep down you have what it takes to give another the love you wish to be reciprocated. I just hope one day you take a chance because even though it's beautiful to be alone, doesn't mean you can't share your love with someone to create something more beautiful. I just hope whoever the woman is, she's perfect. I hope she fits with you, perfectly. I hope she doesn't hurt you. I hope she's secure. I hope she's that 1% you've been searching for through disappointment after disappointment. You deserve the same love you give, and I hope one day, when you find her, you won't be scared to love her.

Don't be scared to hurt her. Honestly, we don't know the outcome of life and whether we're going to hurt anyone, things happen. You must live in the moment, don't worry about what could happen. But don't love until you're ready. If being in your own company makes you feel secure and growing as a person and for your career is best, I suggest you keep going. Just don't be scared to take chances, just make sure whatever it is, it's reciprocated. It's 2:22 right now and I'm still going, I don't plan on stopping for a while so I apologize for this being long but I haven't wrote in a week and you told me to write a piece, so I'm giving you this. Let's talk about everything I adore about you. Let's see, I love your face. It can be the

corniest thing ever but seeing your face
lights up my whole day. And your smile is
one that can't ever be forgotten. I admire
your features. But knowing your heart, and
your dorky personality, one that I can be
me with, makes me feel free. I love being
open with you, I love that I can say
whatever I feel, and you don't judge me.
I've never been this open with anyone
honestly, which may be hard to believe, but
I really haven't. I've never held back
anything when it's come to you, except my
own feelings. But I've held back my feelings
because I know they're not reciprocated and
holding them in just makes it less real.
Sometimes I think I'm crazy for feeling so
much with not even meeting you, and other

times I just feel happy and love how deep I feel for you. It's a unique feeling. Someone who I call my friend, who's an amazing friend, who I have uncontrollable feelings for, who've yet to touch, seems so unreal. But honestly, I've felt you without sex and that's more intimate to me. My heart has connected with you first and that's how I believe this works. Even though I want to make love to you repeatedly like every hour, my heart has connected before that's happened. I don't have one bad thought in my head that things would go wrong, I believe when I see you in 11 days that I will feel exactly the same as I do now. I will look into your eyes and see deep into your soul and there's no coming back from there.

I'm ready for this weekend to ruin my life. I'm ready to become a mess. Because it's going to happen. I've tried to separate my feelings and the real, but I can't seem to. What I feel for you is extremely powerful and sometimes I don't even understand it, but I don't try to analyze it, I just enjoy the feeling, live in the moment and take as much of you as you give me and hope one day we will make our way to each other. So, do what you have to do, be with any women you feel you need to be with, have fun, go out and do whatever your heart desires. But I hope when you think of letting that go, you think of me. But again, that's just me wishing on a daydream and I know daydreams are unreal. I don't want you to want me because I do nice things for

you, because I support you. I don't want

you to want me because you feel as if that

would make me happy. I'm very unsure of

how you feel at the moment and a part of

me hates it but I can't really demand much

because this is a whole mess, and you've

told me the deal, and unfortunately I

caught feelings and I had no intentions on

doing so, because you were incredibly

wonderful it was hard. I do want you to

know that there's no pressure, if this isn't

ever reciprocated, I will be okay. I will be

okay with being your friend. I will be okay

with having you in my life no matter the

case. Because you were a friend to me

before anything else and I feel that's what

matters. I'm sorry if my thoughts are all over the place. But no matter who I try and explain this to, they never understand. Half the time I don't understand, but lately it's became clearer to me and I've been able to understand. I was just scared to put myself out there. But I realize if I don't take a chance I can't complain. These months that I've known you have felt like forever. I've felt like you're the missing piece to my puzzle that I've been longing for, that spontaneous kind of love. Sometimes I get embarrassed because I feel like I'm too obsessed with you, I get too excited just to speak with you or see your face but you're my favorite high. That's why I can't lose you. I'm sorry I get so upset when you question my intentions, but I just wish you

fully understood the love I have for you,

and how much of it I have. How crazy I

am for you, not literally crazy, but you

know. A lot of it I can't explain. Sometimes

all I can do is smile and get butterflies in

hopes I can put words to those feelings. But

I know in time I will. I know whatever's

meant to be, will happen and I'm ready for

whatever that may be. I'm ready to see you

and have the best time of my life and enjoy

your company even if that's the last of it. I

just want you to know, that you are my

favorite person, in real life, and there's no

one else I'd choose. You take all my fears,

all my worries, and every part of me I

looked away from, free.

Thanks for being you. Thanks for being a wonderful friend. Thanks for being amazing. Thanks for writing the best books I've ever read. Thanks for showing your heart to the world and being incredibly adorable. I will forever remember your smile that gives me goosebumps and a face that is admirable. I could stare at you all day and not get tired. I could fall in love, repeatedly. You are perfect.

And I love you, very much.

Letters to you

July

July 2, 2018 8:50 a.m.

*I want to call this piece "the aftermath"
because this is everything I feel at this exact
moment. I just read your last piece I wrote,
and everything is still accurate. I said some
meaningful, insightful things that still
make sense, which I figured would. I'm on
the plane right now heading back home. I
want you to know that leaving you this
morning was incredibly hard, I didn't know
how to take in this whole weekend, I
literally broke down a hand full of times in
the car and at the airport. It was just 3
days ago, getting on the plane getting ready*

to see you, happiness was beautiful, life was amazing. I want to go back to that day first. The anticipation of getting on that plane knowing I was coming to see you, I had no fears, I had nothing holding me back. I know I was coming, I know what I wanted, and I made it happen. I got over one of my biggest fears, well a lot this weekend. I told myself I would never get on a plane, ever in my life. I wouldn't even get on a plane to see my mom when she lived in Georgia. I told my ex I would never get on a plane with him for any vacation. I've surrounded myself with my fears for all my life and I drowned in them, time and time. But for some reason, I had to see you. The universe gave me the "you're safe" green

light and I ran with it. My second fear,
traveling alone. I barely like to leave my
house to go anywhere in town because I get
"people anxiety" I hate seeing locals, I hate
communicating with just about anyone.
But for some reason, you made me feel safe
enough to make this journey. And lastly,
my biggest fear, was meeting you. Before I
came out I thought about it a million
times, I thought how I shouldn't just up
and leave my town to go see some man I've
never met, in a place I've never stepped foot
in. But the ultimate fear wasn't just that,
it was facing all these emotions I've held
inside me, the feelings I've yet to face head
on, in reality. I've been living in my dream
world of you. And I'm not saying that what

we could have couldn't be real, more like I never thought it could. I know I always go back to the past but it's so hard not to think of everything that brought me to this. You were the light that lead me through the darkness, the light I've never thought I'd see. You eased the pain and made walking away from something I didn't even realize was toxic, you helped me get through that milestone in my life very calmly. I've never met anyone like you. Someone who's soul is just the purest form of beauty. Sometimes I never understand why you were so kind, why you dealt with all my bullshit. But you were always there, and always listened, while having all the right things to say. I could have never done any of this without

you. I would have never realized I deserved
more until you helped me see the parts that
needed to be dead and gone. I know you'll
probably take no credit, but I give it all to
you. I do believe I deserve more, and more
as in the best. I do believe I'm capable of
loving myself with the same love I give to
others. I do believe that I will be successful
one day, very successful, along with making
all my dreams come true one day at a time.
But can I tell you, ever since I met you, my
dreams have been aligning perfectly. I know
I made them come true, I know publishing
my first book has nothing to do with you,
that was all me. But every dream after
that, has been inspired by you. And I thank
you, for guiding me in the direction I was

meant to. And I thank you, for being with me through some of the dreams I've always dreamed, watching them come true. I don't believe I "owe" anything to you, as vice versa. I believe the love we share is enough to show why we do the things we do for each other, and that alone is what makes sense. Everything I do for you, showing your work and your heart to the world, is something I never want to be repaid for, because that's something I kindly do, from the bottom of my heart, because I believe in you. I believe in the you that you can be and are. When you drown in self-doubt, I'll always be here to pick you up from the waves. Not because I must, because I love you too much to watch you drown, knowing

you're one of the greatest souls to ever exist.
Sometimes we see others in ways we don't
see ourselves, and that's the beauty in
loving someone, you see them for everything
they are, and love them exactly for that
reason, flaws and all. So yes, I know you're
not perfect, I know you might not be where
you want to be in your life at this moment,
or not as successful as you wish to be, at
this moment. But you are not measured by
how much money you make, or what kind
of job you have, you're measured by your
character and how you show your heart.

Your drive for the dreams you want to
make your reality, the heart you show so
deeply and intimately to the world. We've
all been in a situation where we've been a

burden or failed. I've gotten disappointed times and times again. But what I always had, was my heart, and my character never changed through these situations. I know the things I do isn't measured by the amount of money I make, or the things I can provide for another, I'm not the richest person, but I will spend my last to make sure someone I love has what they need. I've spent money so carelessly, well because, there's always more money. Have you ever just sat down and thought about money? And how stupid it is? The amount of money we waste on the stupidest things? Yeah, it's not worth it. At one time in my life I thought money was important, which of course it is, we can't live without it, but honestly, money isn't happiness. Money is the devil that makes us feel as we're not good enough, like we need to impress people with nice things, but that's not how life works, and that's where people always go wrong, that's why they will never understand true happiness. So, I get it, stability is important to you, to be able to provide for another, and give someone you love exactly what they need. But being stable it's not always about providing, it's about partnering. That's just what I've learned. I don't need you to give me the world, because you are that already. There's no amount of money, or material items that could ever amount to you. That's where I draw the line with funds.

It's 9:26, and I'm still on the plane, enjoying the view, wishing I was back in your city. Let me get back to the weekend. When you texted, me you were on your way, I had to try and process everything at once, "how am I going to deal" was my first thought. Seeing your face in real life was so scary to think, because I knew I would become a mess. I know things didn't happened as I planned, but every time I think of seeing you on the sidewalk passing you my heart just stopped for a quick second, everything I prayed for had become reality, and I wasn't sure exactly how to face it. That moment was so beautiful. I sit here and repeat it over and over in my head and it makes me happy, yet sad at the same *time. I literally cry tears of happiness and sadness at the same exact time and the shit is so confusing. I thought getting on that plane was enough for me to be prepared, until I seen your face and I was lost. I couldn't even look at you because it all felt like a dream. This whole weekend was a dream, one I never wanted to wake up from. A beautiful dream that became a reality, for one weekend, amazing. It was exactly what I wanted, and a bit more. To see you, in the real, was exactly how I pictured you. No fantasyland can beat reality you. You are so much more real than any daydream I've created of you, you are so much more than any fantasy I've created. I wasn't disappointed, not once.*

Everything was exactly how I pictured it would be, and it was all equally amazing. It was all so natural. It felt like we've known each other for years, when it's only been two months. I felt so safe in your presence, and so open to be me, without fear. I've never once felt that in my life. I've always held a little back just to make others comfortable, but you, you make being me so easy, because you're you and you accept me perfectly. You see me for the person I am, and I can't thank you enough for letting me be in your presence this weekend and making me feel whole once again. Not saying I don't feel whole alone, because I'm secure, I'm very capable of being alone. But just because I can be

*alone doesn't mean I don't have a piece
missing that needs filling. You are that
piece. You are the perfect fit. That's all I
keep thinking. All I keep thinking is "why
isn't this possible" if you're the perfect
piece? That's where I'll always get lost.
Maybe that's where I'll end up
disappointed. But at this point,
disappointment is the least of my worries.
I'm just trying to make sense of the mess I
made, the mess I've created within my own
heart and my own head. I know regardless
of what happens between us we'll always
be friends, even though it will be the
hardest thing to do, it's better than having
to live life without my best friend. The one
person who gets me like no one else does,*

and when I say that, I mean it completely.

I've never connected with anyone on this

level, a day in my life. It's a beautiful high,

a high no drugs could amount to. You're

my high. This weekend was the greatest

weekend of my life, now it's a part of a

memory. A beautiful memory. I only hope

to make more memories with you. I only

hope to see you again and enjoy more of

your presence. This weekend proved we

didn't need to do anything, we completely

enjoyed each other's presence and that

alone is a lot to do. I completely enjoyed

doing nothing but talk with you, pure

happiness. From getting to admire your

face, to seeing that beautiful smile, to see

you truly happy, was everything I prayed

for. I only prayed this weekend was nothing less than perfect, and the universe aligned our paths perfectly and I can't thank you enough for giving me all of you this weekend. I can't thank you enough for letting me give you all of me, and you knew exactly what to do with me. I can't thank you enough for going to sea world with me and seeing the whales for the first time and enjoying every minute with me. It's so crazy how you never made anything about you, how you gave that day to me completely, and I've never had that ever, because I'm too much the same and that's exactly my ways of doing. But we balance each other out, and that's beautiful. I'm not sure if I must even talk about the love making, it pretty much spoke for itself, but I adore how it was more than just sex, how you made it more than anything I've ever had, intimately. I never knew talking during sex was a thing until you, and how beautiful it can be. I will miss those moments. Looking into your eyes while you gave me all of you, I found myself deep in your soul, and at times I wanted to break down because I knew that I'd have to disconnect, but I lived how I wanted to in that moment and it was everything. I've been working on the living in the moment instead of picturing the future, and it's been beautiful. I only pray that there will be more one day, because there isn't anyone else I want, and I know I haven't lived, I haven't met enough people to see. But I don't want to, I don't overlook any feeling I get when it's this raw. I have met my soulmate and I promised myself I would never overlook that when I came face to face with it. I know this is a lot of pressure on your part, but please don't feel pressure. I don't want you to feel anything but what you feel. Whether or not we become one, one day, I still have you, and the greatest memories of my life, and I thank you for letting me get the chance to love you, and the chance to be able to experience a piece of life with you.

Watching the office with you, to being complete freaks the next minute, to talking deeply about our feelings, about life, and about everything. You are my best friend, I hope you know that. I admire every part of you. To you singing the whole car ride back to your house, to you being with me to make a dream of mine come true when you could have found something better to do, I admire your soul. I admire you dancing in front of the tv while eating pizza. I could have never imagined someone who was so perfect. I love ALL of you. All "three" of you, equally. I admire how you make me laugh. I admire how you make me smile. I admire how happy I just am, in your presence. I admire the safeness you bring when I'm around you. All my fears, all of my worries, everything didn't matter this weekend, my focus was you, and only you. I know I'll find more to say, but for now, I'm going to go. But please, know that this was amazing. I wish I could have stayed forever. And yes, the future is where it's at, and right now all we have is the moment, but I will pray to God every night that someday, this moment will turn into the future. Because there's no one else out there, that will ever make me feel the way you do. And I say this with completely honesty, you are everything and more, please know that. Please know that you are my favorite person. I love you my love.

July 4, 2018 11:40 a.m.

I have so much to be thankful for, with you being one of them. When you walked into my life it was a dark place, so dark I couldn't even see the darkness. I could only feel something was missing, then you came and aligned everything perfectly. You became so close to me in such a short period of time, and I thank you for being a wonderful friend. I thank you for opening my eyes to the parts of my life I needed to renew. I thank you for letting me find peace within your guidance. Loving me is now something I can do, freely, while truly

*being genuinely happy. Who I am now is
who I've always knew I could be, who I
was scared to be. With you, I'm free. With
you, there's nothing I can't be. I've become
secure, I've become capable of being alone,
while enjoying my own solitude. I don't
know what I've ever done to have someone
like you enter my life, but knowing my
prayers have been listened to, knowing I
have someone like you in my life is the most
beautiful gift I've ever received. I thank
you, so much, for being my light through
the darkest times. For showing me how
beautiful it is, to love myself.*

You are my favorite.

You are loved, I hope you know that.

July 4, 2018 11:51 p.m.

Today, I feel a bit more on the sad side.
I've been on such a high since I left you.
I've been so happy, since I left you. Being
in your presence was something I've wanted
to enjoy for months, and I finally mastered
it. And it was incredible. The way we vibe
is so perfect. I sit and think about that
weekend over and over and wonder how I
could ever enjoy someone so much, as I
enjoy you. I could be around you all the
time, and never become tired of you. But
today, the high doesn't seem to high, I feel
lowest of the lows and I'm not sure why. I

wish I was with you, then here in my own company, and I know I can't be there at this moment, but it's killing me slowly. Life isn't fair. I'm thinking why I had to love someone who was so far, why the universe aligned me with you, knowing life would get in the way. But the craziest part, I'd move my whole life around just to be with you. Just to make it work with you. And that truly scares me. To pick up everything and just go to you. Spontaneous, you make my heart happy, you make my soul feel alive. But you also make me scared, because I couldn't imagine having to be without this feeling, and the scariest part of it all, it's possible. Anything's possible and that scares me.

July 5, 2018 10:38 p.m.

Thank you, God, for always listening.

For never letting me give up.

For giving me the strength,

To never overlook my heart.

Everything I've prayed for,

Is now aligning perfectly.

I can't thank you enough,

For giving me the greatest gift of all.

July 7, 2018 4:25 a.m.

I'm thankful for every girl,

Who chose to overlook you,

I'm thankful,

They weren't meant to fit with you.

Because we were meant to align perfectly,

you were meant for me,

Every part of you,

Was made to fit with me.

You're mine,

Nothing can compare,

To the love we've created.

July 9, 2018 12:32 a.m.

I want to first say, I'm on cloud nine. A feeling I've never once felt, ever in my life, until recent events have shown me that I deserve true happiness. Last year, I told myself that 2018 was going to be my year, the year of putting the pieces of me together and making all my dreams come true. I'm half way through the year and even though I've lost people I thought I'd keep with me forever, I've gained not only a peace of mind, but I've gained the strength to be secure on my own. I've gained the strength to walk away from toxic behavior. I'm *proud of who I've become, and how far I've come. I will never stop soul searching, there's always more to learn about myself. I promise to never let myself get stuck in old situations, but to completely detach myself from the past. I'm a new woman, and everything I want now, is completely different from what I wanted then. I have gained a new perspective on life, and I'm going to love every part of it. I will embrace my love, I will embrace my heart, completely. I will give all of me, or none of me. I have found happiness within my own solitude. I have mastered what it's like to love myself. Now, I can love you, my love. You were the missing piece I've been without, and I'm going to embrace you.*

My love, your love, together we can conquer anything. Thank you for helping me pick up the pieces to my broken self and helping me find me again. You opened my heart, too. You're my balance, I don't plan on living life without you. I've found me, I've found you, I've found us. I couldn't have prayed for anything else, I already have everything I've ever asked for.

July 10, 2018 12:22 p.m.

I'm on my lunch break in my feels, weird, I know. But today is annoying and it shifted my whole mood, so here I am, writing you. I know we've both been broken, we've both had pieces missing for some time now.

Whether you believe that or not, considering when you met me, how could I be missing a piece knowing I had someone? But let me tell you, our problems were long before I met you, it wasn't until I let myself be a friend to you, I clearly seen everything right in front of me. I outgrew him long ago, a part of me just felt like there wasn't anyone else for me. I latched to comfort and I thought that was important. But my soul always yearned for more. I found myself wanting to be alone more than a hand full of times. I wanted my own space more than I wanted his company. Things just never vibe the way I wanted. I found myself tip toeing around certain situations, feelings just to get by without a fight. The kind of love he gave me was only to an extent. The love never grew, it was always the same kind of love when I first met him. We weren't going nowhere together, what I wanted was far more than what he even had for himself. Me writing my first book put a lot of my life into perspective for me, and how I felt, I was just too scared to *walk away. Because I'm too vulnerable when it comes to hurting anyone, I was blinded by what I thought I was being loved with, and I found the comfort and held it close. I was unhappy, but I felt as if I was stuck. And maybe terrified to experience life alone, not knowing if anyone else was out there for me. Before I met him, I had one boyfriend who was serious, my first "love" that was the worst time of my life, but it taught me what love wasn't, but also how hard my heart goes for one I love. I've learned so much about myself with these two. I don't regret giving them my time, even though it might feel like I've wasted years, I've gained so much insight on who I am, who I want to be, and the* kind of love I want one day. I have the strength to love someone with every part of me, because I've finally understood the different parts of love. I've understood how it feels to have someone you love not love you back. I've understood how it feels to love just within your own comfort. I've understood how it feels to settle. I've tried to be okay with it all. But my soul is too strong to settle for someone who doesn't have the fire I do. Who can't love me the way I love them. My soul craves a different kind of love, the kind of love you give me. The spontaneous, welcome "home" kind of love. This is a love I've never felt before, a love that is greater than the other kinds I've experienced. Your love is special, it's

timeless, and it gives me security. Knowing
you were a friend to me before we even
made it here, means you're more than just
someone to me. We built a friendship, a
pure friendship. Even though the force, I
remained quiet, until I thought it was okay
to let how I feel be known. I know it's only
been 4 months, but seeing you, being with
you for just that one weekend gave me all
the answers I needed. Even before I went, I
knew you would be the one. My heart beats
a different way for you. My soul connects
with you without even trying to be anyone
other than me. You get me. You accept me.
You genuinely care. I look into your eyes
and I can feel how real every moment of
happiness is. Everything felt right, and I

knew right there I wasn't letting you go, if I didn't need to. For the first time in my 25 years of living, I finally felt alive. You did that. You gave me the piece of me I've been searching for all this time, I finally feel complete. And I know it sounds crazy, because if we don't end up lovers forever, what does this mean if I lose this piece? But I will never lose you, regardless of what happens between us, I hope you'll always be my friend. I hope you always know you're special to me, in a way that's completely indescribable. You make the moon look average, and you know how much I love the moon. Seeing your face always puts me in a better mood. I admire your drive for success and making all of *your dreams come true. Our energies together, can conquer everything. You match mine. I pray to God every night, thanking him for sending me you, the greatest gift I could have ever asked for. He held you away for a while for reasons, but he couldn't have brought you into my life at the right time. He just knew. I'm so blessed to have you. To share moments of life with you. To get to share my thoughts, fears, every piece of me I was afraid to let free, I can with you. I know we've agreed to live in the moment, which I will, I will completely enjoy each and every moment I have with you and cherish it. But I can't lie and say I'm not thinking about the future, and what could come of us.*

Life has been so beautiful. I've never been happier. I hope you know you've played a huge part in that. I've found myself through the mess I've created, but it all ended up a beautiful disaster. I believe everything happens for a reason, and I'm happy that everything happened exactly how it did. I'm happy I chose you. You my love, are everything I've dreamed of, there's no one out there for me, it's you.

July 12, 2018 10:26 p.m.

You're the missing piece to my imperfect puzzle. You're everything I've been searching for all this time. I can't wait to be with you again, I can't wait to experience the rest of my life with you.

July 13, 2018 2:13 a.m.

It's been 11 days since I last seen you, and for some reason it feels like forever. I've been counting down the days, to the hour and the minute I get to see you again. I had high hopes that when I seen you that weekend, the universe would work in our favor. But going out there, I had a whole lot of emotions I didn't have under control. I went out with an open mind, an open heart, but also a mess of uncontrollable feelings I never expressed clearly. At that point I was confused on how I could feel so deep for a man I never once felt. But for some reason I've already felt you, because when I laid my eyes on you that first time, everything felt as real as I believed it would. When I first laid my eyes on you I felt a rush of happiness, a rush I've never felt go through my body. I had butterflies extremely, I couldn't even look you in the eyes because I was convinced I was living a dream. That moment is my favorite moment of all. The first time I got to witness you, as you are, in the real. Regardless if the moment wasn't what we had originally planned, maybe a little awkward, but I wouldn't trade it for anything. I'm not sure how you felt in that exact moment, but I knew right then I wanted you. I was ready to give all of me to you without hesitation. I gave myself to you at that moment. I've had people tell me "you don't know him, don't go miles away from home to meet a stranger, alone" but you weren't a stranger. You were my best friend. Tons of long night talks on FaceTime, real life conversation. I knew people were just nervous for me to experience since a different kind of experience. Because I'm a woman, and traveling alone can get scary, but I wasn't nervous. Knowing you were on the other side is what held me through it. Knowing I got to see you, made it all worth it. I surprised myself, never would I thought I'd get on a plane. But I loved every minute of it. It was all a beautiful thrill. I would do *it all over again, a million times if that's what it took to see your face. I would do anything. Because that's how hard my heart goes for you, endlessly. As I'm thinking of it now it still all seems like a dream. A dream I was devastated to wake up from. Once Sunday hit, I was completely torn. Torn because I didn't want to leave you. I was so unsure of what would happen when I left, a lot of things were left unsaid, and there wasn't enough time in the weekend to go over everything we felt. But that weekend was all about feeling each other's vibes and understand each other more. That weekend was all about finding the spark that was there, or whether it was or not. This weekend was the first time in my life I've ever just completely enjoyed "a moment" in that exact moment. I didn't worry about anything, I didn't pay attention to my phone, I didn't care to do anything, but share every moment I had with you. Maybe it was because I didn't know if I'd ever get another moment, but I was so caught up in your presence I forgot about worrying about what came next. That weekend was the best weekend of my entire life. Because that weekend started it all, it made every fantasy, every dream, every prayer I've ever made, become reality. I can recall every moment and replay them in my head and just smile because there the greatest memories of my life. I enjoyed your presence without the need of any entertainment, we made our own. I enjoyed laughing with you, while you made me smile every minute I looked at you. I've never met someone so imperfectly, perfect. I haven't found one thing I don't like about you. We all have flaws, I understand there will be things that will annoy me, things you'll do that will probably piss me off, but I don't care. Nothing can compare to how incredibly happy you make me. I found myself just looking at you and thinking "why haven't I found him sooner" "I can't believe I'm here" "I'm so happy I met him" "he's so perfect" If you were wondering what I was thinking when I just stared at you smiling. I've never loved someone's presence as* much as I loved being next to you. The way

you make me feel is the most beautiful

thing in my world. You make me feel

beautiful. You make me feel secure. You

make me feel like being me is important.

You make me feel like we are meant to fit

perfectly. Making love to you was an

experience, pure bliss. Looking into your

eyes as you were deep inside me, I felt you

take my soul, and that's when I knew, I

wasn't letting you go. There's no one that

can compare to you, or the love you give

me. I knew you were the one, even though I

wasn't searching, I stopped looking. Getting

out of a relationship to find myself, which I

did, I let myself find the parts of me I

needed to love you. I wouldn't have done

any of this if I truly didn't believe I was ready. I wouldn't of flew a thousand miles to be with you if I truly didn't believe we'd be here today. The scariest part, was not knowing what the future held for us, let alone that weekend. It was a big risk to take, whether we could be more. But everything with you felt right. Everything felt like home to me. I wouldn't mind making you apart of my life, however that had to happen, I was going to move the sun and moon just to make it happen. I was once told, when you meet that person who makes you soul happy, in a way you've never felt, that's your soul mate. Yes, we have multiple soul mates in our life time, but you, my love, are not just any soul mate. You are THAT soulmate. The one that fits perfectly with me. The piece of me I've been searching for without even knowing. You are the piece I needed to complete the puzzle. I never overlooked you. I never let you go. Nothing felt wrong with you, everything pushed me towards you. The universe has always been on our side, that's a sign right there. This is the 11 piece I've written to you, and for some reason this never gets old. The words flow perfectly on this piece of paper and I can't even begin to tell you how amazing it feels to express these emotions I've held so close to me. So, that weekend was everything. There's so much I can talk about, there's so much little things I've held close to my heart just by watching you, listening to you, and focusing on you. But now, I'm thinking about what's going to come of us. Not too deep into the future, but I want to start by thinking of next month. Counting down the days until I see your face again. Counting down the days until I get to live the rest of my life with you. Missing you is the hardest thing to do, but I'm so happy I have you to miss. I'm happy to be able to miss someone like you, knowing I get to be with you soon. Then I won't have to miss you again, everything will be complete. You're a thousand miles away, but your heart is still near. I miss you so much, my love. I can't wait to see you. I miss your face. I miss your lips. I miss your touch. I miss your comfort. I miss your dick. I miss your smile. I miss you. I can't wait to show you how much. I can't wait to start my life with you. I can't wait to take over the world with you. We are going to be great. We are going to be, everything. Our love can conquer everything, remember that. The love you give me is a love I'll never find within another and that's special. I don't plan to ever look in another direction, because what you give to me is far stronger than any connection I can come close to. God brought you into my life exactly when he knew I needed you. God brought me into your life exactly when he knew you needed me. We need each other, we balance each other, beautifully. I'm so ready.

I'm so ready to live in every moment with you and fall in love with you every minute I look into your eyes and feel our souls connect. I'm so ready to see what's on the other side for us. I'm so ready, to give you all of me and hope you never hurt me. As I won't ever do anything to hurt you, you're too precious to me, to ever let you go. When I'm with you, there's nowhere I'd rather be. When I'm missing you, there's no one I'd rather miss. There's no one out there who will ever come close to you, you're the reason I'm not just living, you're the reason I'm alive again. You opened my heart, fully, to the point I never knew I could love this much. You've opened parts of me I've kept hidden for years. Your love makes me feel like I can do anything, including loving you with my whole heart. I'm ready to be yours, all yours. As I'm ready for you to be mine. I'm ready for us. I hope to live in this moment forever.

"*God, please protect him from the pain of anything that's out to get him. Please keep him healthy, happy, and forever loved. Please show him that who is his, is someone who deserved to be loved, with the love I have to give. Please make sure he knows how special he truly is. Because I plan on making this last a lifetime, and I just pray he's ready for it. Because there's no one else I'd rather spend every day with, than him. I give you my word, God, I promise to never do wrong by him. By giving him my heart,*

I'm giving him all of me, knowing I can be broken at any time. I'm giving him the same energy I want reciprocated. I promise to never hurt him, but only protect him from the world when it's a dark place. I promise to save him from himself when he's in need of it. His love makes me feel like I can do anything, and I will give him everything. So please, God, can you protect us. I need you to make sure we're good. Because I don't ever want to lose this kind of love. I don't ever want to wake up one day and lose this. I pray that this will always make sense, that we won't ever have to look the other way, because we'll find new ways to fall deep in love over and over, for eternity. Amen"

I love you, Michael. I hope you feel that. Because I only have more to give, and I'm ready to give you all of me.

July 13, 2018 1:03 p.m.

I crave a love that's deeper than the ocean,
a love that's beyond the moon.

I crave the love that's inspired by you.

July 14, 2018 2:36 a.m.

Your love makes me feel like every fear,
every worry, every little thing that once
mattered, is no longer a thought. Your love
makes me feel secure. Your love makes me
feel beautiful. Your love inspires the love
within me, and that's the kind of love I've
always prayed for.

July 15, 2018 9:45 a.m.

I usually only could write masterpieces when the sun goes down. The best when the moon was out, but your love, inspires me all the time. Your love gives me the inspiration to write whenever I feel the rush. I needed this release since yesterday, but I couldn't exactly pin point the exact feeling to put into words. I was overjoyed. I was anxious. I was so happy. We've been "public" for three days now, and the affection you've been giving me, and to the world of me, is something I've never felt so strongly. It was a lot to go public, but at the same time, I've been ready for this since I have seen you. Because that moment was enough for me to be with you. I admire the fact we've waited. I admire the fact we were friends for a while before we mutually decided this. I feel you on a deeper level because of our friendship. The foundation of our relationship will always be conditioned because we know each other without being one. We know each other's story, and we're still learning. But I knew the parts of you I needed to know, as you did of me. Even though we don't have crazy pasts, we both have one, and we both survived each other's. And that's a lot right there to do. You stuck by me through part of mine, you always remained a true friend even when you didn't have to. As I, was there for you supporting you the most because you deserve the world. It was my instinct as a friend to give you the love and support you deserved, it came to me naturally and I couldn't help it. I knew there were reasons we met, I knew there were reasons we came about how we did. I tried not to analyze much, even though times drove me crazy when it came to points I couldn't pinpoint. But everything makes sense now, and I couldn't say anything more, then I'm blessed to know God answered all my prayers. That the universe was on our side this whole time, and how everything is a beautiful miracle.

We both found each other, regardless of our situations at the time, God knew we needed each other. Our love was meant to find each other. Your love was the missing love I've been in need for, since I was searching years ago. But we go through test runs, and failure after failure. Disappointment after disappointment, just to end up here. I'm so happy to end up here, with you. There's nowhere I'd rather be. I'm glad I got to witness the parts of love that I didn't fit with, the love that taught me what I needed to do, to fix parts of myself to love you. We both are great now, we're both in a better place, mentally, emotionally, and secure. There's always more to work on, but within ourselves, we both have what it takes to open our hearts and love other with the love we've been wanting to share. You are that one. You are my soul mate I've been missing. The part of my heart that no piece ever fit, because it was only meant to fit for you. Thank you, for giving me that piece to complete my puzzle. Thank you for giving me the chance to love you, to experience a piece of life with you. Every moment of it was beautiful. I reminisce a hundred times a day just counting down the days until I get to be in your presence again. This time, for as long as lifetime. Because I'm going all in, giving you all of me, I hope you're ready. Which I know you are. I feel every part of us get closer as the days pass, and

I'm so blessed, to get to have someone like you show me what love truly is. I'm only eager to learn more of you and love each part of you more and more. I'm only eager to experience every part of life with my best friend and make the best moments. This time, I'm living within the moment of every special experience with you, because every moment with you is something I want to be within for a lifetime. There's no such thing as memories, only moments. Moments I'll always remember and feel every time I think of you. Every time I look at you, I see the love I've always dreamed of. Every time I look in your eyes, I see the reciprocated love. Every time I touch you, I feel the closeness you bring. The comfort.

The security. Everything about you, brings me happiness. There's no way I'm letting you go, I've waited too long to find you.

July 15, 2018 1:07 p.m.

If I had to choose my favorite thing about us, it would be our openness. Our communication and how we can talk for hours about anything and just vibe, and totally get each other. That's how I know the foundation we've built can't be broken.

July 15, 2018 2:26

The love you give to me, along with the love

you inspire within me, is the kind of love

I've been praying for my whole life. Your

love sets all past love to shame.

July 16, 2018 1:48 a.m.

I always find myself awake this late, while you're already asleep, I stay awake and think of you. Write of you. Not that long ago, I was up this late dreading the sleepless nights, I was a complete mess trying to figure out why the nights were the worst times. But ever since you've brought me light, I haven't seen another dark night. I haven't felt any ounce of saddens pass through my body, except for the fact I'm missing you like crazy. Distance is one hell of an asshole. The thought of being next to you drives me crazy. The thought of looking into your eyes and seeing your smile, I melt because all I have are visions of what that weekend was like. I only have thoughts of the moments we shared, as I'm yearning to be next to you again. In 24 days I'll be reunited with you, and I'm overwhelmed by the happiness I'm going to be feeling when our eyes meet again. I'm going to embrace you tightly and never let you go again.

July 16, 2018 12:19 p.m.

Sometimes I write more than once, in the
same day. Sometimes I can't help but to
release these emotions I hold so close to me.
Some days it's easier to get by, some days it
feels like it gets harder. I've been in a long
distant relationship once before, but the
feeling doesn't amount to how badly I want
to be close to you. I know you might feel as
if our fire will burn out once we're finally
together, without time to miss each other,
but that's false. I will no longer have you to
miss, but I will have you next to me. That's
a win, to me. I would rather you every day

then to crave your presence knowing I can't

have you. Every day will be a new day,

every day will be a new experience. I

promise you, nothing will ever get old.

Nothing will ever get "comfortable" because

when we're together, my soul is alive and

there's nothing I wish to do more, then to

experience every piece of life with you. To

show the world how I'm proud to have

someone who's so special, as you are. This

is just the beginning my love. The beginning

to forever. We have so much to experience,

there's no way I could get tired of you.

There's no way I'd chose to have you 1,185

miles from me, then to be right next to me.

This isn't something that could go out, our

flame, will never burn out. What we have

is stronger than anything that could be compared to anyone. We both know what we feel, we both know that this won't ever get boring. I can't wait to look into the same eyes every night before I close my eyes, and the same face I wake up to every morning. I can't wait to not feel the loneliness we both feel as we lay down at night, because we'll be there to hold each other. There's so much more bliss in having you near, then having you far. My heart beats harder for you every day, and that moment I met you, it stopped for a second, because I knew right then you were the person I wanted to spend the rest of my life with.

So, I'm speaking it into existence.

Letters to you

I want this.

I want this now.

I want this when I see you.

I want this forever.

I just hope you want this too.

July 17, 2018 12:40 p.m.

Sitting here reminiscing about our first encounter. Sitting here thinking about that whole weekend, thinking about my favorite moments. It's hard to decide, because they were all special. But there were moments you've opened my eyes, and those are the moments I can't forget. The first moment, was the moment I saw your face, for the first time. Everything flashed before my eyes, everything from my past was out of sight, out of mind. You were the moment, the moment of truth. The moment I've fantasied about long before we've met, and

115

for that fantasy to arrive, I was far too anxious I couldn't complete a whole thought. I could just smile and try to make sense of what was happening. As I reflect, I've capture the moment in a deeper way, I've realized that I was like a cute innocent girl meeting her crush for the first time, without knowing how to act. Pretty embarrassing, but it was the cutest moment. That moment when I first time I met you, but it wasn't like that, it was like we were picking up we're we left off, years later. It was odd to feel so comfortable with you, to not feel anything but safe in your presence, as I knew nothing but what you've told me. That's how I knew I was in good hands, your energy gave me everything

I needed to trust you. You never once made me uncomfortable, instead you made me feel at home. That was a feeling I'll never forget. My second favorite moment was the moment you left for 4 hours and came back. We've been anticipating seeing each other for months, so to know I was in your city, what was 4 hours? You'd think nothing right? But the moment you came back after being out, the energy was wild. That's the kind of energy I know will forever be there. That spark of love that comes from missing you, even though you just seen me, and we were only apart for not long. In that moment we made love so beautifully, to an album I'll cherish forever. To this day, it's on repeat. It helps me feel closer to you. Making love to you is intensely beautiful, it's more than sex. It's true intimacy, and our connection sets the fire to it all. Out of all the times, that was my favorite moment. My third favorite moment was the moment you laid your head on my chest to intentionally listen to my heart. In that moment, I knew how perfect you were. For you to care to listen how my heart beats for you, is something more beautiful than the words "I love you". In that moment it was racing, because no one has ever thought to listen. No one's ever cared to know. But you, you're the missing piece to my heart and it knew. In that exact moment, I knew there wasn't anyone who was more for me, than you.

There are so many moments I've taken with me, I've cherished. But the best part, there's so many more to come. I am so in love with you, I'm in love with the thought of our future and where we're headed. Being with you has brought me so much light towards what love truly is, I've gained a new experience how to be happy, but to not lose myself trying to love you. You let me be me and love you as well. I thank you, for being someone so amazing. For being the man, I could fall in love with, and letting me fall, just to catch me.

July 19, 2018 7:16 a.m.

I'm so in love it's overwhelming beautiful.
I can't take my brain off you.
I'm so blessed to have such an amazing
feeling come over me,
and I'm so happy you give me that feeling.

July 20, 2018 1:04 a.m.

I just got off FaceTime with you about 20 minutes ago. As we said goodnight, you told me to rest too. But my love, I can't rest when all my brain does is think of you. I've had a rough night dealing with nonsense from someone who felt the need to post my work but not credit me. And the first thing I needed, was your face. Your face puts all my worries at ease. Your face makes everything feel incredible. I could look into your eyes and not once feel uncomfortable. I could look into your eyes and see every

121

part of your soul and that will just take me deeper. I love how we both balance each other, when we're both at our worsts, we make each other be known of our bests, and not let the moment of self-doubt, or someone trying to sabotage us. Even when we're both feeling our worsts, somehow, we manage to pick each other up. You're always there when I need you, and I give you my heart when it comes to anything you need of me. I give you my heart when I seen you that first time. I give you my heart repeatedly. You treat it so gentle and I know it's in good hands. I'm missing you a little extra today, and I did so much yesterday, so much I felt the lowest of lows. Lowest I've felt since we've decided to be together. All I've felt lately was beautiful. But yesterday, I felt like my whole world was crashing down and I couldn't save it. But I stopped and realized, that wasn't the case. I was just being dramatic, and not having you near was becoming an annoying problem. But again, you made me feel at ease. You made me feel as if nothing could ever make me feel anything less than happy. This distance is making me crazy and I know you say it's important to keep our minds off it, but how's that truly possible? When your miles away and my heart literally yearns for your love close to me. It yearns for your touch, your smile, your face. I yearn you. I crave you. And this, isn't going to get easier until the day I arrive in your city, ready to take you back home with me. I can't wait to take you home. I can't wait till we create a home and start our future. I'm so blessed to have met you, and that God sent someone as amazing as you. I can't wait to see you again.

Enclosure,

I chose to stop here. I've written 21 letters all from the moment I met you, until this very moment. There's so many emotions I feel, so many feelings that are real. But, I'm going to end this here, until volume 2. I want people to want more. I want them to have a taste of our love and wonder what comes next. I want them to feel every word I've left on these pieces and feel the parts of me I let be free with you, as you gave to me. I want everyone to understand this is what true love is, and that there's someone out there for everyone, it just doesn't happen overnight, and sometimes it happens after years of being with the wrong person. But the key to it all, is to never give up. To always give all of you no matter the situation, if you feel it's real, give your all. I never overlooked you and look where we are now, look what we've become. Looking back, I honestly never truly could have told you we'd be here. Honestly, I thought we would of just been friends for the rest of our lives. I always thought the feelings would just be one sided, never reciprocated. But honestly, I always felt you had something more for me, but you were too scared to open, so I didn't give up. What we have, is something far from amazing than anything I could have imagined or dreamt of. You are every wish, every dream, every prayer.

You are the man I've prayed for every night before I closed my eyes. The man I've always wrote about when I wrote about finding my soul mate. Our love outshines everything that could try and steal our light. Our foundation is strong. Our love is everything, and as overwhelming as it can be, I couldn't have asked for someone better for me. The love you reciprocate to me, the affection you show me, and the way you show me to the world, is everything to me.

I've prayed for you, now I'm praying I never lose you. I'm praying we'll always make sense, and you won't ever find a reason not to love me. I pray we'll always have this, because you're my best friend, you're the man of my dreams, but now my reality, my world. I'm so blessed, to have you. Please, know that my love runs for you, deeply, and I couldn't ever give that love to someone else, nor would I even want to. You're enough for me, every part of you, is enough for me. I can't wait to learn more of you. I can't wait to fall in love with every part of you. I can't wait to experience life with you. You made a huge decision to move here and be with me, and I couldn't be thankful enough, that's the biggest thing anyone's ever done for me. But it's not about me, it's about us. It's about our love, thank you, for taking a chance with me. Thank you for trusting me that I won't break your heart. I promise, I won't fail you. I won't do anything to hurt you.

Your heart is safe with me, I promise.

You're too perfect, you're too much of a

blessing, and I love you too much to let you

go. I'm in this forever, my love. Until I die,

I'm yours. I can't wait for our future.

Most importantly,

I can't wait to conquer the world with my

soul mate.

I love you, to forever, and even after

forever, I'll still love you.

My love for you won't ever die, even when I

do. This kind of love is for eternity.

Our love is the greatest blessing I've

received. I will thank God every night, for

blessing me with you.

19 days until we start our future.

Meet me to forever babe.

I love you.

I love you so much.

This one's for you.

With love,

Sara

Letters to you

Him

For Sara

To the perfect stranger from afar

Who has yielded more support

Than those who are close to me

your heart beats hard enough

To shift mountains

Yet still holds the softness of a raindrop

In an industry filled with ego maniacs,
manipulators, and users

Letters to you

I've found you, a writer who supports

without an agenda

A human with a humble spirit

And a woman with words that's genuine

I appreciate you

Honestly

Truly

Your soul is filled with inspiration

In which you pour into the world

And I thank you for being you

I thank you for understanding

As I can say without a doubt

You are my first true author friend

Letters to you

.

If you're interested in seeing more of my

work,

Twitter: @moonssoulchild

Instagram: @moonsoulchild

Also, check out his work,

Twitter: @michaeltavon

Instagram: @bymichaeltavon

To be continued. .

Made in the USA
Columbia, SC
01 June 2021